DATE DUE

Classifying Insects

ANDREW SOLWAY

Heinemann Library
Chicago, Illinois

Originated by Dot Gradations
Printed in China

07 06
10 9 8 7 6 5 4

Library of Congress Cataloging-in-Publication Data
Solway, Andrew.
    Classifying insects / Andrew Solway.
        p. cm. -- (Classifying living things)
Summary: Explains what insects are and how they differ from other animals, with an overview of the life cycle of a variety of insects, including ants, bees, cockroaches, grasshoppers, dragonflies, and butterflies.
Includes bibliographical references (p.) and index.
    ISBN 1-4034-0849-1 (lib. bdg. : hardcover) -- ISBN 1-4034-3346-1 (pbk.)
    1. Insects--Classification--Juvenile literature. 2. Insects--Juvenile literature. [1. Insects.] I. Title. II. Series.
    QL468 .S66 2003
    595.7--dc21

                                                    2002015403

Acknowledgments
The publishers would like to thank the following for permission to reproduce photographs:
p. 4 Oxford Scientific Films/TC Nature; p. 5 Oxford Scientific Films/Alastair Shelley; pp. 6, 11, 14, 2(27 Oxford Scientific Films; p. 7 Oxford Scientific Films/Mantis Wildlife Films; p. 10 (left) Nature Picture Library/Mike Wilkes; pp. 10 (right), 17, 18, 20, 21 (bottom), 24 Warren Photographic and Kim Taylor p. 12 Oxford Scientific Films/Michael Fogden; p. 13 Science Photo Library; p. 15 Oxford Scientific Films/Chris Perrins; p. 16 (top); Digital Stock; p. 16 (bottom) Science Photo Library/Claude Nuridsany and Marie Perennou; p. 19 Oxford Scientific Films/Keith Ringland; p. 21 (top) Oxford Scientific Films/Brian Kennedy; p. 22 Nature Picture Library/Dietmar Nill; p. 23 (top) Corbis/Gallo Images; pp. 23 (bottom), 29 Digital Vision; p. 25 Planet Earth Pictures/Geoff Du Feu; p. 28 Nature Picture Library/Michael and Patricia Fogden.

Cover photograph of a large white butterfly, *Pieris Brassicae*, reproduced with permission of the Bruce Coleman Collection/Kim Taylor.

For Harriet, Eliza and Nicholas.

The publishers would like to thank Catherine Armstrong, museum educator, for her assistance in the preparation of this book.

Every effort has been made to contact copyright holders of any material reproduced in this book. Any omissions will be rectified in subsequent printings if notice is given to the publishers.

Some words are shown in bold, **like this.** You can find out what they mean by looking in the glossary.

Contents

The Variety of Life

Insects are a vital part of our world. People often see them as pests, especially when they eat food crops or invade our homes. But without insects, many plants would not be able to **reproduce**. And plants are the basic food providers for all living things. Insects also play an important part in turning dead plants and animals into fertile soil. Also, insects make useful products such as honey and silk.

Scientists can identify more than a million different **species** of insects, and they believe that there are millions more yet to be found. Such a huge variety is bewildering. To try and understand insects better, scientists classify them, or sort them into groups.

You can find insects in every corner of the world. Tiny insects such as this ice bug live on ice and snowfields high in the mountains. Insects like this have special "antifreeze" in their bodies that keeps them from freezing in the cold.

Sorting the living world

When you sort things, they become easier to think about and to understand. Scientists try to classify living things in a way that shows how closely one group of animals or plants is related to another. To do this, they compare groups of living things with each other. They look at everything about a living thing, from its color and shape to the **genes** inside its **cells**. Then they use all this information to sort the millions of different living things into groups.

A species is a single kind of animal or plant, such as a honeybee or a buttercup. Species that are very similar to each other are put together in a larger group called a **genus** (plural genera). Genera that are similar to each other are grouped into **families**, and similar families make up larger groups called **orders.** Closely related orders are grouped into **classes**, classes are grouped into **phyla,** and finally, phyla are grouped into huge groups called kingdoms. Plants, for example, make up one kingdom, while animals make up another.

Scientific names

Many living things have a common name. But when scientists classify living things, they give each species a two-part scientific name. This name is the same all over the world. The first part of the scientific name is the genus that the creature belongs to. The second part is the species within that genus that the creature belongs to.

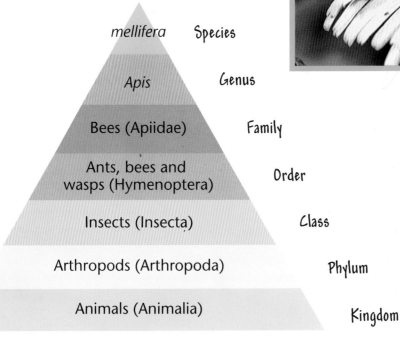

mellifera	Species
Apis	Genus
Bees (Apiidae)	Family
Ants, bees and wasps (Hymenoptera)	Order
Insects (Insecta)	Class
Arthropods (Arthropoda)	Phylum
Animals (Animalia)	Kingdom

This diagram shows the full classification for Apis mellifera—a honeybee.

Animals with Jointed Legs

Insects are part of a **phylum** of animals called the **arthropods.** Arthropods do not have bones. Instead they have a tough outer skin called an exoskeleton. They move around on jointed legs. Crabs and shrimps (crustaceans), spiders and scorpions (arachnids), and insects are the most important arthropod groups.

Scientists believe that the ancestors of the arthropods were a group of worms called the annelids. Earthworms are modern annelid worms. Like annelid worms, an arthropod's body is divided into sections or **segments.**

Body armor

An arthropod's exoskeleton is similar to a suit of armor. It is made up of hard, protective plates connected by flexible joints that allow the animal to move. The exoskeleton supports the arthropod's body and protects its soft insides.

The exoskeleton is a fixed size. It cannot grow with the rest of the animal. This means that every so often an arthropod has to shed its exoskeleton. This shedding process is known as **molting.** A new exoskeleton forms underneath, so when the old one splits, the animal is ready to climb out of it. For a short time, the new exoskeleton is soft. While it is soft, the arthropod swells up to give itself growing room.

Unlike other arthropod groups, insects do not grow and molt once they become adults. This cicada is emerging from its pupa.

Six-legged flyers

Insects are different from other arthropods in several important ways. Crustaceans are mostly ocean-living animals, but nearly all insects live on land. An insect's cuticle, or skin, is covered by a layer of waterproof wax, which prevents it from drying. Insect eggs also have a waterproof outer coating.

Many insects have wings, and winged insects are the only arthropods that can fly. Their ability to fly allows them to live in habitats that other animals cannot reach. For example, insects are often among the first animals to arrive when a new island rises from the ocean.

Unlike other arthropods, an insect's body is divided into three parts: the head, the **thorax,** and the **abdomen.** An insect has three pairs of legs, all of which are attached to the thorax.

Insect power

Insects are the most successful group of living things on Earth. Nearly three-quarters of all **species** are insects. There are about 200 million times more insects than there are people!

Although insects are small, wings allow them to migrate long distances. Monarch butterflies, such as those pictured here, migrate nearly 5,000 miles (8,000 kilometers) each year, from Canada to northern Mexico.

Insect Orders

There are 28 different **orders** of insects. Some, such as cockroaches, have changed very little since the first insects appeared about 300 million years ago. Other orders, such as flies, appeared later.

This table shows a selection of insect orders.

Type	Order	No. of species	Example
Wingless insects	Bristletails (Archeaognatha)	250	bristletail
	Silverfish (Thysanura)	330	silverfish
Insects with incomplete metamorphosis	Mayflies (Ephemeroptera)	about 2,000	March brown mayfly
	Dragonflies (Odonata)	about 5,000	green clearwing dragonfly
	Cockroaches (Blattodea)	about 3,500	American cockroach
	Termites (Isoptera)	about 2,200	drywood termite
	Mantids (Mantodea)	about 1,800	praying mantis
	Earwigs (Dermaptera)	about 1,200	earwig
	Grasshoppers and crickets (Orthoptera)	over 20,000	desert locust
	Stick and leaf insects (Phasmatoidea)	about 2,700	pink-winged stick insect
	Parasitic lice (Phthiraptera)	over 3,000	human louse
	Bugs (Hemiptera)	about 67,500	bedbug
Insects with complete metamorphosis	Lacewings (Neuroptera)	about 5,500	lace wing
	Beetles (Coleoptera)	about 300,000	stag beetle
	Scorpion flies (Mecoptera)	about 475	scorpion fly
	Fleas (Siphonaptera)	over 2,200	oriental rat flea
	Two-winged flies (Diptera)	about 90,000	Crane fly
	Caddis flies (Trichoptera)	about 10,000	caddis fly
	Butterflies and moths (Lepidoptera)	about 150,000	peacock butterfly
	Ants, wasps, and bees (Hymenoptera)	about 280,000	leaf-cutter ant

Life cycles

Nearly all insects hatch from eggs, but different types of insects develop in different ways. The changes an insect goes through during its life are called **metamorphosis**. In some insect orders, such as dragonflies and grasshoppers, the babies look similar to the adults when they hatch from the egg. At this stage they are called **nymphs**. As the nymphs grow and **molt**, they gradually develop wings and become more like adults. This kind of life cycle is called **incomplete metamorphosis**.

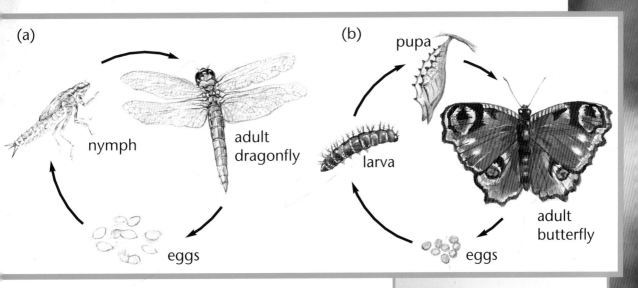

(a) nymph / adult dragonfly / eggs

(b) pupa / larva / adult butterfly / eggs

The babies of insects such as butterflies, flies, and bees are very different from the adults. They are called **larvae**. A larva is an eating machine. As it eats, it grows and **molts** several times, but it does not change to become more like an adult. It just gets bigger. When the larva reaches its full size, it molts one more time and becomes a **pupa,** or chrysalis.

The pupa does not feed or move. It is surrounded by a hard protective case. Inside, an incredible transformation takes place. The larva turns itself into an adult insect—a wasp, fly, or butterfly. This kind of insect life cycle is called **complete metamorphosis.**

Metamorphosis *means "change." Dragonflies change gradually as they grow from eggs into adults. This is called incomplete metamorphosis (a). Butterflies, on the other hand, change in stages, from an egg to a larva (a caterpillar) to a pupa to an adult. This is called complete metamorphosis (b).*

Insect wings

The very first insects had no wings. A few close relatives of these early insects are still found today. There are also some insect **species** that once had wings but no longer have them. This happened because they live underground or in tree trunks, for example, where they do not need wings.

Many insects have two pairs of wings. But in some insect groups, one pair has been **adapted** for some other purpose. In beetles, for instance, the front pair of wings has become a pair of hard, protective wing cases.

Beetles

There are more types of beetles than of any other living thing. They are the largest **order** of insects. Ladybugs, weevils, fireflies, and woodworms are all beetles.

What is a beetle?

All beetles use only their hind wings for flying. The front wings are hard, armored wing cases that cover the beetle's back. The hind wings fold away under these wing cases.

The type of mouthparts, or jaws, an insect has depends on what it eats. Most beetles have biting mouthparts, but some feed in different ways. For instance, some beetles suck up the food. Their mouthparts have been **adapted** to suit different ways of feeding.

*An Onthophagus African dung beetle rolls away a ball of dung it has gathered. Dung beetles belong to the scarab beetle **family.** There are more than 7,000 species of dung beetles.*

As a ladybug flies away, its wing cases swing forward and its wings open.

Beetle feeding

Beetles live and feed in a huge variety of places. Some, such as ladybugs and tiger beetles, are **predators.** Farmers and gardeners like ladybugs because they eat insects such as aphids, which can damage flowers and crops. Other beetles feed on plants. Leaf beetles eat leaves, while woodworms and deathwatch beetles eat wood. Weevils are plant pests. Many of them eat important farm crops.

Many **species** of beetle are scavengers. Some eat dead leaves and rotting vegetation, while dung beetles eat animal dung. This might not sound very appetizing, but these beetles play a vital part in turning animal waste into rich, fertile soil.

Finding a mate

Adult beetles need to find a beetle of the opposite sex in order to **mate** and produce offspring. Different species do this in different ways. Female chafers and click beetles produce a special scent that attracts males. Male fireflies produce light, which they use to signal to females at night. Most female fireflies cannot fly. They glow in response to the male's light, and the males drop down to mate.

Adult stag beetles feed on sap and honeydew. Only the males of the species have enlarged jaws that look like horns or antlers.

In some beetle species, males fight each other for the chance to mate with a female. Male stag beetles and rhinoceros beetles, for instance, have large horns that they use to try and tip each other over.

Ants, Bees, and Wasps

The main thing that separates ants, bees, and wasps from other insects is their "wasp waist." Part of their **abdomen** is very thin and flexible. Some ants, bees, and wasps are social insects and live in large colonies. But many **species** also live alone.

Parasitic wasps

Many wasp species are **parasitic.** Their **larvae** feed on or inside other plants and animals, eventually killing their **host.** They then become **pupae** and hatch as adults.

Parasitic wasps lay their eggs on or in all kinds of plants and animals. The many species of ichneumon wasp, for instance, are parasites of the larvae and caterpillars of various insects.

Solitary wasps and bees

Many species of wasps and bees are solitary. They live alone and only meet with other wasps to mate. Solitary bees and wasps dig small nests for their eggs and gather enough food to feed their larvae from birth to adulthood.

Some parasitic wasps lay their eggs in or on other animals. Many species lay their eggs in caterpillars. This caterpillar is host to parasitic braconid wasp pupae.

The long egg tube of bees and nonparasitic wasps has become a stinger. Solitary wasps use this to kill their **prey.** Solitary bees collect **pollen** and **nectar** to feed their larvae. They make honey from the nectar and fill the nest with honey and pollen.

Social ants, wasps, and bees

Ants, and some wasp and bee species, are social insects. They live in large nests with a queen who lays all the eggs, and many female workers who find food and look after the larvae. There are also a few males. Their job is to mate with new queens. In some ant species, large soldier ants guard the colony.

Ants dig their nests into the ground or pile up soil and other material in an anthill. Bees and wasps build nests in holes or on trees. Bee and wasp nests contain combs made up of many six-sided cells. Larvae are raised in these cells, and the combs are also used to store honey.

Not all ants are predators. Leaf-cutter ants grow their own food. They cut small pieces from leaves and carry them to their nests. There a fungus grows on the leaves. This fungus is the ants' main food source.

Cockroaches and Termites

You can find cockroaches (**order** Blattodea) almost anywhere. They live in deserts and swamps, on mountains, in cold areas, in burrows underground, in trees, and in caves. Some **species** live alongside humans in cities and towns.

Termites (order Isoptera) are closely related to cockroaches. They live in large colonies made up of millions of termites.

Cockroaches

Cockroaches have a flat body, long antennae, and a hard plate that protects the head and front of the body. Cockroaches often are found in places where humans live. Their flat bodies fit into all sizes of cracks, where they hide during the day. At night they come out and scavenge for food.

When female cockroaches lay their eggs, they cover them in a sticky liquid. This liquid hardens to form a tough protective case. Some species of cockroaches carry the egg case around with them until the eggs hatch. The newborns are tiny **nymphs** that look similar to the adults.

A cockroach's digestive system contains millions of tiny creatures called protozoa, which help it to digest its food. It can even eat tough materials such as wood.

Termites

Termites look somewhat like large-headed ants, but they do not have a "wasp waist." Most feed on dead and rotten wood. Like cockroaches, termites have tiny creatures called protozoa living in their guts. These help them to **digest** tough food such as wood.

A termite colony is started by a termite king and queen. Once the first termites are grown, they take over raising the babies, leaving the queen to concentrate on laying eggs. She swells and swells until she is a huge egg-laying factory, producing more than 30,000 eggs a day.

There are several kinds of termites in a colony. Most are workers, which feed the **larvae,** find food, and build the nest. Soldiers defend the nest from enemies. Some soldiers have huge jaws, while others have a snout that produces a horrible chemical spray. Other, winged termites fly off to set up new colonies elsewhere.

The nests of some termite species are wonders of architecture. Some African species build huge mounds more than 23 feet (7 meters) tall. The mounds are chimneys, which draw hot, stale air out of the nest. The nest itself contains galleries full of termite larvae and food stores, where the termites grow a kind of fungus found only in these nests.

Australian compass termites build tall nests that are broad on one side and narrow on the other. The broad side faces the morning sun, so the nest warms up quickly. The narrow side of the nest faces the midday sun, so the nest does not get too hot.

Butterflies and Moths

Butterflies and moths belong to the same **order** (Lepidoptera). They are the only insects that have thousands of tiny scales covering the surface of their wings. Often these scales form beautiful patterns and colors.

A Pandora's sphinx butterfly feeds on a flower. The long tongues of butterflies and moths mean that they can reach the nectar in deep, tubular flowers.

Most butterflies and moths feed on **nectar** from flowers. They have a long, flexible tongue that they use to suck up nectar, similar to juice through a straw.

Patterned wings

In some butterfly and moth **species,** the bright patterns on their wings are a warning that they are poisonous. These colors also help butterflies to recognize their **mates.**

A butterfly or moth that is not poisonous cannot be brightly colored, because it will become easy food for a **predator.** So some species have secret markings that are visible only to animals that can see ultraviolet light. Butterflies can see this type of light, but their enemies cannot.

The feathery antennae of a male giant peacok moth (Saturnia pyra) can smell a female moth up to 3 miles (5 kilometers) away.

Metamorphosis

Butterflies and moths are the best-known examples of **complete metamorphosis.** Butterfly and moth **larvae,** or caterpillars, feed on plants.

Caterpillars are slow-moving and make a tasty snack for a bird or lizard. Luckily, they have various ways of avoiding being eaten. Some use **camouflage** to hide themselves. For instance, many looper caterpillars look like twigs. Other caterpillars are brightly colored. This warns predators that they are poisonous or are covered in itchy hairs or spikes.

Once a caterpillar is fully grown it becomes a **pupa,** or chrysalis. Pupae have a hard outer case or a silk **cocoon** that protects the changing insect inside. When the adult emerges from the pupa it is no longer a wormlike caterpillar but a winged butterfly or moth.

Feeding

Like bees, butterflies and moths are flower specialists. Their long tongues allow them to reach a flower's nectar that is too deep for other insects to reach. Nectar is almost pure sugar. Because animals also need protein in their food to repair and renew themselves, most adult butterflies and moths can live for only a few weeks. But a few live longer, because they feed on protein-containing **pollen** as well as nectar. The zebra longwing butterfly, for instance, lives for up to six months.

Some very tiny caterpillars feed inside leaves, leaving white tracks in the leaf called leaf mines.

Air Acrobats

As their name tells you, two-winged flies have only one pair of wings. But they are not poor fliers. They can fly backward, hover, turn on the spot, and even land upside-down. The secret to their flying skill is a pair of structures, called halteres, just behind their wings. Halteres look like balls on stalks and are actually the remains of the fly's hind wings. They help the fly to balance in flight. Only two-winged flies have halteres.

halteres

*In this picture of a Crane fly you can see the fly's halteres. Most flies have good eyesight. Their huge **compound eyes** do not give as clear a view of the world as our eyes do, but they are better at spotting movement.*

Fly larvae

Female flies choose a place to lay their eggs that will help their **larvae** find the right food when they hatch. If the larvae eat plant-eating insects, for instance, the female lays her eggs on plants where these insects might be found. Other fly larvae are **parasites.** Botfly larvae, for instance, live just under the skin of large animals such as sheep. The female fly lays her eggs on the animal's skin, and the larvae burrow under the skin when they hatch.

Fly food

A fly's mouthparts form a tube that the fly uses to suck up liquid food. In some cases, the food is already liquid, but the fly can also pump saliva, or spit, onto the food, which turns the solid food into liquid.

Many kinds of flies are scavengers. As with beetles, scavenger flies are important for breaking down dead animals and plants to produce rich, fertile soil.

Some flies get their food from dung. Male dung flies gather around a fresh pile of dung, looking for females. When a female arrives, she **mates** with one of the males. Then she lays her eggs in the dung.

Other groups of flies, such as midges, mosquitoes, and horseflies, are bloodsuckers. They feed on the blood of large animals. But it is only the females who drink blood. They need protein from the blood to make their eggs. Males of these **species** feed on **nectar** from flowers.

Many other flies get at least part of their food from flowers. Hoverflies feed only on nectar. Their yellow and black stripes make them look like bees or wasps, but they are harmless.

Robber flies can catch and kill insects bigger than themselves in mid-air. They stab the victim with their piercing mouthparts and inject poison.

Disease-carriers

People do not like some kinds of flies because they are disease-carriers. In hot countries, mosquitoes carry tiny protozoa in their blood that cause the disease malaria. In a similar way, tsetse flies carry a disease called sleeping sickness. If an infected mosquito or tsetse fly feeds on a human, it may pass on the disease.

Bugs

People often call any small insect a bug. But in scientific term bugs are a large, varied **order** of insects with mouthparts tha form a stiff, thin "beak." They use this beak for piercing and sucking up food. Most bugs feed on plant sap.

Bugs are divided into two groups based on the differences in their mouthparts. True bugs include brightly colored shield bugs and water bugs such as pond skaters. The other group includes aphids, cicadas, and treehoppers. Treehoppers look bit like grasshoppers, but they are not related to them.

True bugs

Part of the front wing of a true bug is hard, but the rest is clear and flexible. No other insect has this kind of wing. Bug can swing their beak forward to feed, which means they can feed on other things besides plant juices. A few bugs, such a pond skaters and assassin bugs, are **predators** that feed on other insects.

Another thing that separates true bugs from other insects is that they have stink glands on their **abdomen.** If a predator comes too close, the bug sprays it with a foul-smelling liquid from these glands.

Shield bugs are sometimes called stinkbugs because of the smell they leave on plants that they have been feeding on.

Hoppers, cicadas, and aphids

Unlike true bugs, hoppers, cicadas, and aphids can move their beaks to only the vertical, or up and down, position. All of them feed on plants, piercing through the outer surface to the juicy sap beneath.

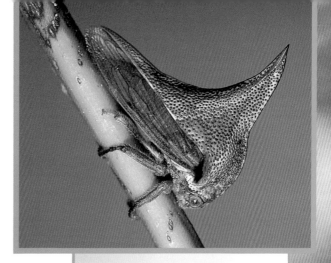

The best-known hoppers are frog hoppers and spittlebugs. The **nymphs** of these bugs produce a frothy white substance known as cuckoo spit. This protects the nymphs from drying out and from being attacked by predators.

*Some treehoppers have strangely shaped bodies. Some **species** look like thorns when they rest on plants.*

Cicada nymphs live underground, feeding on the sap of roots. Some live underground for seventeen or eighteen years. Adult cicadas live above the ground, but only for a few weeks. Male cicadas make a high buzzing or hissing song to attract females.

Aphids are tiny insects that feed on plants in large colonies. Some aphids are pests to farmers and gardeners because they damage or sometimes kill the plants they feed on, and their numbers can grow incredibly fast. When food is plentiful, all aphid babies are born female, and they do not need to **mate** to produce eggs. Each aphid can produce three to six babies per day. The babies grow very fast, becoming adults within a week.

Aphids produce a sweet, sticky substance called honeydew as a waste product. Insects such as bees and ants love to eat this honeydew.

Grasshoppers and Crickets

Grasshoppers and crickets are medium to large insects with strong back legs that are good for jumping. All grasshoppers and crickets make sounds, and they also have ears to hear sounds. Their front wings are hard, to protect the large hind wings, which fold up like a fan does.

Grasshoppers and crickets eat plants, but many will also eat animals. A few **species,** such as the mole cricket, are mainly **predators.**

Grasshopper lifestyles

Some grasshoppers and crickets live in the open, while other live mainly underground or in caves. Grasshoppers and crickets that live in the open have long bodies. They protect themselves from predators in various ways. Some species are **camouflaged.** They may be colored in such a way that they are almost invisible when still, or they may look like twigs or leaves. Others are poisonous or produce bad-smelling liquid when attacked. These species often have bright warning colors.

Grasshoppers and crickets that live underground have shorter bodies and powerful front legs that they use for digging. Some species feed on the roots of plants, while others eat microscopic creatures in the soil.

Grasshoppers and crickets can be divided into two groups: long-horned and short-horned. This is a bluewinged grasshopper, Oedipoda caerulescens. *Its long back legs and sail-like wings can be clearly seen.*

Locust swarms

Most grasshoppers and crickets live alone. But some species that live in hot lands change their behavior when there is plenty of food. They gather in huge swarms by the billions. These insects are called locusts.

Singing and dancing

Like cicadas, male grasshoppers and crickets sing to attract a **mate.** They make sounds either by rubbing part of their back leg against their hard front wing or by rubbing their front wings together. The sounds they make can be loud. In fact, the mole cricket has a way to make its song even louder. It digs a specially shaped burrow that amplifies the sounds so that it can be heard up to one mile (two kilometers) away.

Locust swarms can cause enormous damage to food crops. Swarms can contain as many as 40 billion insects. Swarms this large can block out sunlight.

Surprise attackers

Mantises are close relatives of grasshoppers and crickets. They are also related to cockroaches. Mantises are large insects with a triangle-shaped head. They are predators and masters of the surprise attack. Many species look like leaves, twigs, or flowers. They hold themselves absolutely still, with their large front legs up. When a suitable victim comes near, the mantis shoots out its front legs and grabs it. The legs are covered in hooks and spines to help hold the **prey.**

Mayflies and Dragonflies

Dragonflies and mayflies are two of the oldest **orders** of insects. They first appeared flying over ponds and swamps about 300 million years ago. That's about 70 million years before the first dinosaurs!

Both mayflies and dragonflies have long, slender bodies and two pairs of wings that cannot be folded away. The young **nymphs** of both groups live underwater and breathe through gills as fish do.

Adult mayflies live only a few days, just long enough to breed and lay eggs. They do not eat at all. Their abdomen is filled with air, which helps them fly better.

Mayflies

You can often find mayflies around ponds and streams in the summer. They are medium-sized insects with large front wings and smaller hind wings. Three long bristles or tails stick out from the end of their **abdomen.**

Mayfly nymphs live in streams and ponds, either swimming freely or burrowing into the stream or pond bed. The nymphs live underwater for up to three years. They filter tiny pieces of food from the water or find food in the mud.

Just before the nymph is fully grown, it crawls out of the water. It then **molts** and becomes a dull-colored adult called a dun. This is not the true adult. The dun flies only a short way before it molts one more time, now becoming a true adult.

Male mayflies gather in swarms and dance above the water. Females are attracted to these swarms and **mate** with the males. They then lay their eggs in the water.

Dragonflies

Dragonflies are bigger than mayflies and are often brilliantly colored. They have large eyes and short antennae. Like mayflies, they are often found near water. Both as nymphs and as adults, dragonflies are fierce **predators.**

Dragonfly nymphs live in all kinds of watery habitats, including under waterfalls and in pools of water in large tropical leaves. They have powerful jaws, which they can shoot out to grab **prey.** They live underwater for up to six years before coming out of the water and molting.

The new dragonfly adults spend a few days or weeks hunting away from the water before returning to mate. When they are fully mature, males are often brilliantly colored. The males of some **species** help with the egg-laying, holding on to the female as she lays her eggs on or near the water.

Dragonflies like this one hunt in the air. They use their excellent sight to spot their prey, and then they grab it with their spiny legs.

The first dragonflies

In the past, dragonflies were even bigger than they are today. Around 300 million years ago, some dragonflies had a wingspan bigger than a duck's wings!

Fleas and Lice

Have you ever had head lice? People often get them at school. They make your head itch and can sometimes be hard to get rid of. You are less likely to have had fleas, but you may have a pet dog or cat that has had them. Lice and fleas are not related, but all **species** in both **orders** are **parasites.** They ride around on mammals or birds, feeding on their blood or skin.

Lice

Lice are highly **adapted** to their parasitic life. They are tiny, wingless, dull-colored insects that have a flat body and short legs. They have strong claws, which they use to hang on to their **host.** Their mouthparts are either piercing or chewing. Some lice feed on small pieces of skin, but many species suck blood.

Lice live their entire lives on their hosts. Most simply hang on to fur or feathers, but curlew lice live in the hollow stems of the wing feathers, while pelican lice live in the pelican's throat pouch.

Female lice fasten their eggs to the host animal's fur or feathers using a hard, quick-drying "glue." The young lice that hatch from the eggs look similar to the adults. They **molt** three times before they are fully grown.

A human louse, Pediculus humanus, *climbs up a human hair.*

Fleas

Fleas live in a similar way to lice, but they look very different. While lice are flat from top to bottom, fleas are flat sideways. This makes it easy for fleas to move around through fur or feathers. All fleas have piercing and sucking mouthparts. Some live on their hosts, but others live in the animals' nest or burrow. Fleas jump onto their host when they want to feed.

Fleas lay round, smooth eggs that fall to the ground. When the eggs hatch, blind, wriggling **larvae** emerge and feed on the dried droppings of the adult fleas. Once fully grown, each larva spins a **cocoon** and becomes a **pupa**. An adult flea can stay inside the cocoon for up to twenty weeks, waiting for a host animal to come by.

The biggest difference between fleas and lice is the way in which they move around. Lice walk, but fleas can jump twenty times their own height. They use this jumping power to get on and off their hosts.

This is a rabbit flea, Spillopsyllus cuniculi. A flea's body is covered in backward-pointing bristles and spikes that help it to stick to its host. A hungry flea looking for food can jump 600 times every hour.

Is It an Insect or Not?

Not all creepy-crawlies are insects. As you have learned, insects are only one type of **arthropod**. Other arthropods also have a hard outer covering and jointed limbs. It is sometimes difficult to tell arthropods apart. Spiders, woodlice, centipedes, and millipedes could all be confused with insects.

Scientists have found several key differences between insects and other arthropods. By looking at all the differences together, it is possible to tell whether an animal is an insect or not.

Count the legs

One difference between insects and other arthropods is the number of legs they have. Insects have 6 legs (3 pairs), while spiders have 8 legs. Woodlice have 10 to 14 legs, and centipedes and millipedes have between 20 and 400 legs.

However, counting legs is not helpful for insect **larvae.** Caterpillars can have up to ten "false" legs as well as the six jointed legs that will become adult legs. Other larvae, such as those of two-winged flies, have no legs at all.

Millipedes, such as this giant red millipede, have two pairs of legs on every segment of their body. Their close relatives, the centipedes, have only one pair of legs per segment.

Body parts

Insects have three parts to their bodies: a head, **thorax,** and **abdomen.** In some cases it is possible to see that the thorax and abdomen are made up of several **segments.** Spiders have only two parts to their bodies: a combined head and thorax and an abdomen. The body of a woodlouse has 12 or more segments, while the bodies of centipedes and millipedes are divided into as many as 100 segments.

What kind of eyes?

Many insects have **compound eyes** that are made up of thousands of small eyelets. Most other arthropods have simple eyes, which are similar to our own. Spiders have eight simple eyes. In many spider **species** these eyes are small, because most spiders rely on touch and sound rather than on sight. But jumping spiders and wolf spiders have very good eyesight, and two of their eyes are bigger. Most centipedes and millipedes have two simple eyes, although some have no eyes at all.

*Jumping spiders are **predators.** They crouch in wait for their victims, then leap on them when they come within range.*

If you were just going by their eyes, you might think that some species of woodlice were insects, because they have compound eyes. However, counting the legs or segments of a woodlouse would show you that it is in fact not an insect.

Glossary

abdomen lower part of an insect's body

adapt to gradually change to fit into a habitat

arthropod animal with an outer skeleton and jointed limbs

camouflage color, shape, or pattern that disguises an animal against its background

cell smallest unit of life. Most animals are made up of millions of cells.

class level of classification grouping between phylum and order. Insects make up a class.

cocoon covering of silk spun by some insect larvae when they become pupae

complete metamorphosis change of an insect from larva to pupa to adult

compound eye eye made up of many small, simple eyes working together

digest to break down food so it can be used by the body

family level of classification grouping between order and genus

fossil remains of ancient living creatures (usually formed from bones or shells) found in rocks

gene substance by which all living things pass on characteristics from one generation to the next

genus (plural is **genera**) level of classification grouping between family and species

host animal or plant that an animal lives in or on

incomplete metamorphosis change of an insect from a nymph to an adult

larva (plural is **larvae**) insect baby

mate to come together to make babies; or, an animal's partner

metamorphosis change

molt to shed the outer skin

nectar sweet liquid produced by some flowers

nymph young stage of an insect that undergoes incomplete metamorphosis

order level of classification grouping between class and family

parasite living thing that lives and feeds on or inside its host, which is another living thing

phylum (plural is **phyla**) level of classification grouping between kingdom and class

pollen powder produced by flowers that helps them reproduce

predator animal that hunts and eats other animals

prey animal that is hunted and eaten by another animal

pupa (plural is **pupae**) hard protective case or cocoon where an insect larva turns into an adult

reproduce to have babies

segment part of an animal's body

species lowest level of classification grouping. Only members of the same species can reproduce together.

thorax middle part of an insect's body, between the head and abdomen

More Books to Read

McEvey, Shane F. *Bugs.* Broomall, Penn.: Chelsea House Publishers, 2001.

Parker, Steve. *Adaptation.* Chicago: Heinemann Library, 2000.

Wallace, Holly. *Classification.* Chicago: Heinemann Library, 2000.

Index